It's Going to Be AUlright

Testimonies from Ausome Women Raising Ausome People

Presented by: April Green

Contents

Dedication

This book is dedicated to the memory of Gerry, a beautiful soul who was suspected to have been living silently with autism and endured struggles in the face of ignorance, stigma, and lack of support.

This book is dedicated to all of the ausome moms, dads, grandparents, teachers, siblings, loved ones and friends that love someone living with autism.

Loving someone living with autism teaches you how to love in a different way. It teaches you how to love unconditionally, and it teaches you how to appreciate the little things most people take for granted when it comes to raising a child to adulthood.

When caring for a person living with autism, every milestone seems to turn into a wondering. I wonder will my child talk, I wonder will he be able to drive, live on his own, transition to work, navigate the community independently? Will they be able to have a relationship, get married, have a family?

Oftentimes the wonderings turn into a source of stress, anxiety, and cycles of grief. This book is dedicated to helping people move from pain to peace to purpose knowing that in the face of challenges associated with autism, It's Going to Be AUlright

Acknowledgements

I would like to give honor to my Lord and Savior Jesus Christ for first planting this vision within me and giving me the strength and courage to step outside of myself in order to move in my purpose.

A random idea, or so I thought, turned into a mission driven by my journey from pain to peace to purpose as my husband and I walk the path of raising three ausome people living with Autism Spectrum Disorder.

Through the journey, I have truly learned that God does not call the equipped, He equips the called.

Thank you to Catherine Hughes our editor and contributing author for all of the energy, dedication, and passion poured into and that continues to be poured into the project which has now turned into a worldwide movement.

To Kita Stewart-Thompson, I thank you for speaking life over this project. Thank you for seeing purpose in this vision in such a fervent way.

Catherine and Kita have truly been the wind beneath my wings and I thank God for equipping them - for through their talents and gifts, I have been equipped.

To Dr. Nicole Barber, thank you for all of your encouragement and for pouring into this vision in such a powerful way.

To the ausome group of women - Christina Abernethy, Jennifer Bruno, Kelly Cain, Donna Lund, Patti McCloud, Sarah Parks, LaJuan Poole, Anne Shipps, Holly Teegarden, and Lenore Wossidlo - thank you. Thank you for not being afraid to tell your stories, bringing encouragement and hope to others as they navigate their journey with autism, while bringing awareness to the many aspects of the disorder and its impact on those who love them.

Jeremiah 1:5 NIV
"Before I formed you in the womb I knew you,
before you were born I set you apart; I appointed
you as a prophet to the nations."

Preface

You.

Sit, close your eyes for a moment, and breathe in deeply. Hold it, and then breathe out. Repeat. Now, hear my words well. Beautiful soul, stop being ashamed that you are tired. We are here to rejuvenate you. Please stop feeling empty. We are going to fill you with energy and love. Do not believe the lie that your life is over.

Your next season is around the corner - and so is your loved ones.

You all are destined for greatness.

The angels are coming. God has tested you all. I know. He tested me too. All three of my beautiful children, my gifts from the Lord are diagnosed on the autism spectrum. But from what I once thought of as a mess, I have discovered His message.

Like me, you may have been born from, or have been experiencing later in life, a journey of pain. I … we … are here to share with you our stories and let you know that your journey can move from pain, to peace, to purpose.

I had a vision for creating a book that is encouraging - one that helps parents and caregivers (especially women just like us) to feel less isolated by showing them a tribe of people who care and who "get it."

We all need to find "our people." We hope you identify with us and that we become "your people" when you feel like no one else is around. When you feel alone and that "no one is here for me," I promise you, we are.

Our world can never have enough efforts that promote awareness, acceptance, inclusion and love. We can never share enough stories. Maybe hundreds, if not thousands, of stories have been shared across the world through the media, blogs, books, shows and more about journeys through autism. You haven't heard ours.

Through our words, we hope to embrace you, to guide you, to motivate you, and ultimately transform you. It is our hope that you, in turn, will unapologetically share your own story and that you will never stop aiding your loved one(s) to find their own voice, and bless others with your family's words.

With love and peace,

April Green

Foreword

Data shows that 1 in 59 children have been diagnosed with an Autism Spectrum Disorder (ASD) according to the CDC's Autism and Developmental Disabilities Monitoring (ADDM) Network (Centers for Disease Control and Prevention, 2018). These statistics only begin to emphasize the importance of early detection, efficient and culturally sensitive treatment modalities, as well as access to services and resources. In doing so, autism can continue to obtain the credibility for an increase in behavioral health services and medical care as well as research endeavors.

These efforts will broaden our understanding on the integrative supports rendered to individuals diagnosed with ASD. These services target common behaviors such as poor social skills, aggressive behaviors, ignored instructions or requests, an inability to communicate effectively, what we commonly call "tantrums" (which manifests differently in every person), or self-injurious behaviors (for example, hitting one's head). Therefore, it's important to implement the proper treatment modalities to address these symptoms. For instance, Applied Behavior Analysis (ABA), backed by five decades of research, is well-known and beneficial through employing obtainable goal setting, structured routine, concrete instructions, modeling, shaping, and task-oriented behavioral plans. Hence, the individual has the opportunity to experience accomplishing milestones.

Furthermore, other commonly utilized approaches such as music or the arts, speech therapy, occupational therapy, nutritional supports and structured social skills groups are all credited as extraordinary assets to the overall emotional well-being of the individual. It should be strongly recommended for the individuals and immediate family members or caretakers to participate in the development of an ongoing treatment.

When intervention is implemented appropriately and respectfully, no matter how impacted by their diagnosis, one can learn how to

7

become invested in their treatment, take pride in who they are, and feel a sense of control in their life.

With treatment, education, and a village behind them, the significant voices of people identified with autism will be empowered. In hindsight, it's their voices that reshapes our world view, our faith and our understanding of humanity. These strong voices embark on adventures only understood by few - and we are looking to change that.

Hence, they encourage us to cross cultural boundaries to seek resolutions, to dismiss distortions of individual differences and to embrace each day with hope. It is this hope that challenges society to acknowledge the human rights of all in the pursuit of equality. Therefore, we all are joined together as one and are contributors to this life.

Life has taught ⌐t it does not unfold the same way for everyone. A per ⌐ to soar above the obstacle or to live beneath th⌐ ⌐al that autism can draw out from each ⌐ ⌐ to demonstrate unconditional ⌐yond expectations. ing guidance to ⌐ the answer to ⌐ ⌐s for forging cʰ ⌐le to conceive.

These ⌐ ovide us with c⌐ ⌐he life of some⌐ ⌐ggles and trium ⌐elmed, the prof ⌐ for insight and the ⌐ ⌐, these brave souls are on the ⌐ ⌐s and those of their loved ones. Thereto⌐, ⌐o respect their path and their story.

As an aunt of a child diagnosed with ASD, it's rewarding and insightful. I am privileged to learn that love is multifaceted, but yet unique. It's constantly changing from encounter to encounter. But it never loses its purpose nor its dedication. It does not stop because of a mishap or repeated offense or misunderstanding or fear of the unknown. Instead, love proceeds with courage knowing I've been chosen to be in his life. I've been chosen to share in his trials and joys. It's me that God selected to pray for and to care for him when needed. So, I become more committed when he speaks one word, then two words and finally blurts out a full sentence. In such a moment, a smile comes across my face and I come to realize the hidden treasure stored behind gentle eyes. He trusted me to share his thoughts, frustrations and happiness. Truly, I am honored that a child has taught me some key principles for life. For example, his journey is teaching me not to be afraid to live, that patience is a virtue, that forgiveness offers freedom, to boldly ask for what you want and to approach each day with hope.

In conclusion, this book collaboration project was orchestrated by a God inspired individual, April Green. I'm fortunate that our paths that crossed in church quickly revealed a passion for advocating for the rights of individuals diagnosed with autism and/or a comorbid mental illness. She has established an essential platform to discuss the real life issues surrounding autism. It is her authenticity, compassion, and tenacity that will continue to heighten the awareness of ASD. This lady of valor has a unique gift and true calling that can't be duplicated to minister to a much needed community.

Undoubtedly, April's motherly wit and acquired knowledge of autism will transform lives forever.

~ Dr. Nicole Barber

Meet Dr. Nicole Barber

Nicole C. Barber's spiritual journey developed during her youth and adolescent years as she attended the First Baptist Church located in Harrisonburg, Virginia. On May 8, 1994, she professed Jesus Christ as her Lord and Savior. Her spiritual journey continued to unfold as she was licensed as an Associate Minister on September 29, 2001 and ordained as an Elder on April 25, 2006.

In accordance to her educational pursuits, she has over 26 years of experience working with individuals diagnosed with mental health, trauma, familial, and spiritual dilemmas. She is a licensed clinical professional counselor (LCPC) who is responsible for overseeing a psychology department providing primary mental health services to inmates diagnosed with serious mental illness, substance abuse and/or personality disorders as well as traumatic history. In May 1992, she obtained her Bachelor of Arts degree in Psychology from Norfolk State University. In May 1996, she obtained her Master of Arts degree

10

in Counseling Psychology from Towson University. She continued her studies at Loyola College where she obtained a Certificate of Advanced Studies in Pastoral Counseling in May 2001. In May 2005, she graduated from Howard University School of Divinity obtaining her Master of Divinity degree. Gratefully, she obtained her doctorate in Pastoral Community Counseling at Argosy University in June 2016.

Moreover, in 2008, she wrote her first book, A Restored Vessel: A Guide to Overcoming Trauma to provide an in-depth and candid perspective about underlying matters surrounding sexual abuse and domestic violence.

Nicole has conducted many workshops, including Behavioral Disorders in Children & Adolescents: Integrating Christian Principles for Effective Outcomes; Mental Health Awareness; Spirituality in Health Care; Trauma, Integrative and Spiritual Practices in Mental Health; Crisis Intervention; and Intimate Partner Violence.

Breaking the Silence
Christina Abernethy

*"Listen to God in the silence of your heart and
you will know His perfect plans for you."*
~ Psalm 37:4

Nonverbal. I remember hearing those words and thinking, "what does that even mean? What do you mean my son is nonverbal?"

A thousand things running through my head ...

Will he ever talk?

Will he be able to say Mom and Dad?

Will he say I love you?

A hundred different emotions filling my soul, and the strongest of them all was fear.

What if he doesn't ever talk?

What if he can't communicate?

What if he never says a word verbally?

What does that look like for him? Or for our family?

I was so scared and worried about the future. The thought of the unknown started to consume me. It would take my breath away the longer I thought about it. I knew I couldn't stay in that mindset and that I needed to act quickly.

So I took all of my emotions, and I have turned them into purpose. I knew we had to get our son help to speak. Even if he can't say words verbally, he needed the tools to help him communicate!

We started with sign language and also enrolled him in speech therapy. I knew how beneficial both could be for our son, so we started right away. We incorporated sign language videos to help us learn how to sign, and he soon loved it! We would watch the videos and learn new signs together as a family. It was amazing!

As he grew older and verbal speech was still not present, his speech therapist introduced picture cards. He was able to point to pictures and let us know when he was hungry or if he wanted a drink. From there, they recommended a speech device, or as we call it "a talker." Alongside speech therapy, we were also encouraging him to communicate with us through pressing buttons on his device. In time, Ethan (our "Bubba") was able to say "eat," "drink," "play," "dinosaurs," and more with his talker!

As time went on, Ethan would press a button on his "talker," and then he would try to repeat it! For example, he would hear "apple" on his speech device and say "ah!"

It was so awesome to watch him in action, but most importantly, to finally hear his little voice.

Whether we were signing or using his device, we never stopped verbally repeating the words, too. It's always been very important to us to be consistent and keep in mind that the big goal is for him to communicate fluently with verbal speech.

Ethan's device and signs continued to encourage his speech development. However, it was still a struggle to truly understand and know what he wanted or needed, when he wanted or needed it.

It is so hard as a parent to not know how to help your child. Do you know what that feels like?

If you're shaking your head yes right now, please know that you are NOT alone!

To feel helpless ... to not know how to help your child ...

Are they in pain?

Are they sick?

Are they scared?

Are they nervous?

It's like a guessing game, and you're really never sure if you're right.

But no matter what, we refused to give up hope. We would never stop trying new things that we thought might help our son communicate.

Years of trial and error, ups and downs, lots of tears, and then one day ... there it was. "Mom."

Wait, what?! Did he just say that? Did my little boy just say "Mom?!" Did that word just come from our Bubba?

YES, IT DID! And then, he said it again!

"Mmmmmmmoooooooooooooooooooooooooooomm!"

The sweetest sound I've ever heard in my entire life happened that day in our living room. It was a day I wasn't sure would ever come, but fully believed that it would! I will never forget the excitement in his face. I will never forget the happy tears and our entire family clapping for him. His brother and sister both hugged him tightly. Celebrating the moment together made my heart explode! It was a day our family will cherish forever.

Just a few weeks later? He said "Dad!" I've never seen my husband's face light up with so much joy.

I knew from that point on that he still has so much more inside of him! I can see it in his eyes and I can see how badly he wants to communicate with us. I started looking for something more, something we haven't tried that might be THE key. That one class or that one therapeutic approach that will help him soar!

I am very active in the autism community, and I enjoy being a part of groups and helping other families! I also enjoy learning from other parents and getting ideas of new things to try or therapies to research. I had heard about music therapy, but I didn't understand exactly what it was.

Was it like a music class? Does it teach children with different needs how to play instruments? Does your child listen to different types of music and it's therapeutic to them? I had no idea, but I definitely wanted to learn more and to see if it was something we could try with Ethan!

After doing some research, connecting with friends, and calling different programs, we found one that we thought would be perfect for our Bubba! We enrolled him in classes. His music therapy sessions are 30 minutes long, and they incorporate music as a means of helping children to talk, learn, play and engage in social situations. They also learn colors, their ABCs, numbers and shapes all while playing music and singing songs that the child loves! They even do a little dance sometimes (which Bubba just loves).

Every session is different and changes for each child. They base the sessions around your child's needs or wants on that particular day, which is individualized and amazing.

Since day one, they have sung a "hello" song at the beginning of the session. The music therapist will play her guitar and sing "hello hello hello," then our son is supposed to answer back "how are you?," and then together they will sing "it's time for music."

Bubba would sit and smile or he would dance along to the guitar while his therapist sang. We were a couple months into his sessions, and one day, she starts singing and playing her guitar:

"Hello hello hello..." she sang.

From Ethan's lips, we heard: "How are you?" This is the part where I practically fell off of my chair and started ugly crying. I went running over to him to give him the biggest, proudest mom hug and kiss ever! I even considered hugging the music therapist because I was just so happy and excited for him.

Three words ... THREE words! In. A. Row.

I still get goosebumps thinking about it and now sharing it as I type this excerpt of our story. This boy never ceases to amaze me! He works so hard day in and day out just to be able to do things that come so easily to others, but he NEVER gives up.

Autism has taught me to never take life for granted. It has taught me to treasure every milestone and goal accomplished, no matter how big or small. It has taught me strength and patience that I never knew I had. It has taught me to never give up hope, and never lose sight of what's truly important in life. It has shown me that autism is a part of our son, but it does NOT define him. Autism is just a part of our sweet, funny, silly little boy who loves dinosaurs and trains!

Our journey is far from over, and there is still hard work to be done. We will continue to guide him and support him every single day no matter what it takes! I know with every ounce of my being that our sweet Bubba will be able to have conversations with us some day. He's already come so far, and has worked tirelessly to get where he is today. We have spent years trying to help him find and use his voice.

Every single therapy session, every appointment, and every meeting is truly worth it and I would do it ALL over again.

Always remember, you are not alone and never give up!

It's never, ever too late to … break the silence.

Meet Ausome Mom Christina Abernethy

Christina is a dedicated wife, mother of 3, and passionate activist for people impacted by disabilities. She has coordinated events to fund research, supports and service dogs for families. She has served on local committees, coached an adaptive cheerleading team, and won awards for successful fundraising endeavors including those for "Team Bubba," honoring her son with autism. She is the founder of Love, Hope and Autism and is proud to be the coordinator for Changing Spaces Pennsylvania, a movement to build accessible restrooms with adult sized changing tables across communities to promote inclusion. She is working with legislators to pass a bill in Pennsylvania that would require such facilities in hospitals, airports, museums, rest stops, malls and more. Christina is committed to spreading a message of heightened awareness and acceptance of differences, ultimately inspiring hope. For her efforts, she won the Achieva Excellence in Family Supports Award in 2018.

Cassie's Voice
Jennifer Bruno

"Anyone can give up. It's the easiest thing in the world to do. But to hold it together when everyone would understand if you fell apart ... that's true strength." ~ Chris Bradford

For any parent or caregiver of a child with autism reading this, you know how much of a mental and emotional struggle it is to take your child to an event or activity that is not a part of your normal routine. You imagine every possible scenario in your head, knowing very well that you will be thrown some sort of curve ball that you didn't see coming.

You second, triple and quadruple guess yourself and talk yourself out of going at least 10 times before you finally put on your big girl pants and venture out into this sometimes cruel world.

What was intended to be just a quick trip to a high school swim meet to support our neighbor at her senior night, turned into one of my worst nightmares.

I knew attending would be hard for Cassie. She is visually impaired AND she has autism, so I knew it was risky to take her to a pool. She would smell the chlorine and think she could swim. It would be echoey and very humid; all of the ingredients for a perfect storm. It was all of those things, just like I knew it would be. But my older daughter insisted that going was the right thing to do. She said that our neighbor would be so happy that we were all there for her. Cassie has very few "friends," but the kids in our neighborhood are all so accepting of her and she loves all of them.

So we did the thing I knew we shouldn't do.

19

Now let me clarify, I had never been to a swim meet before this night. I didn't know if there was swim meet "etiquette" but I became concerned with Cassie's typical outbursts during the diving portion of the meet. I even turned to my neighbor sitting next to me and said "we are going to get kicked out of here because Cassie is going to cause someone to slip off the board and hit their head."

I tried giving Cassie my phone to listen to music or one of her favorite stories to keep her occupied, but my older daughter said it was too loud. I tried giving her earbuds, but she wouldn't leave them in her ears.

I also want to clarify that she was NOT yelling non-stop. She was excited and maybe a little anxious because this event was out of the norm for us. She would yell out every so often. Of course, many athletes and spectators stared (which I am used to when we go anywhere) but at this point in our journey I am able to ignore almost all of it.

Immediately after the senior recognition portion of the meet, we were approached by one of the coaches and the site administrator. I was told that the coach from the opposing team was concerned that Cassie's outbursts may cause one of his athletes to false start but that we were welcome to go stand in the hallway and watch from the window.

I honestly don't remember if I responded. In my 15 years of being a parent, 13 years of which were spent raising a child with special needs, I have never felt more isolated, humiliated, and embarrassed as I did at that moment. I grabbed Cassie's cane and we left the pool area.

We were followed by four of the other neighborhood students, my older daughter Carly, our adult neighbors and a few other adults who were standing near the door. One of these adults happened to be a former employee of our district and she said "We all love Cassie. Everyone that works with Cassie loves her. I can't even believe this is happening."

I don't know for sure that any of the neighborhood kids fully comprehended what transpired, but what I witnessed over the next hour was one of the most special moments I can recall in my adult life.

Students were in tears because Cassie was asked to leave. They were saddened by the fact that Cassie was singled out and treated differently because of her challenges. These youths ranged in age from 11-15, an age group where I think most kids normally gravitate to the mean side or bullying rather choose compassion.

They were hurt.

They were angry.

This happened in OUR school district - the district where Cassie should be considered "one of their own;" the district where I send both of my daughters each day with the assumption that the administration will not only educate my children, but advocate for them and look out for their well-being.

I choose to believe that everything that happens (to me, anyway) for a reason. I made the decision to attend this swim meet. The fact that we were asked to leave the pool area after the senior recognition portion was God's way of nudging me to tell my story and educate communities so something like this might never happen to another family.

Right, wrong or indifferent, I reached out to some folks I know who broadcast for one of the local news stations in Pittsburgh. I went live on Facebook and told my story from start to finish.

My "job" as Cassie's mom is to make sure this world is as accepting of a place as possible for her, when I can no longer portray that role in her life. I take that responsibility more serious than any other role I have ever played. I will always be her voice in a place where she does not have one. I will defend my actions to include her in any and all activities that she deserves to be part of fully and unquestionably. If this means that I have to make someone "feel bad" because "they have never dealt with autism before," then that's what I will do, even though my intention is just to educate.

If you are reading this book and you don't have a loved one on the autism spectrum, let me try to express this in a way you will understand and ask some questions. Do you have a "typical" child? Do you have even a pet? Think back to when your child was an infant and the only way to communicate was through crying. As a new parent, you had no idea why your baby was crying, right? If you have a pet, when your pet is not acting as they normally do, they have no way to tell you what is wrong, correct?

Welcome to life every day for those of us with a child on the spectrum who struggles with effective communication. As parents, we do the best we can with what we know and what we are given. We make gut decisions and we hope and pray that they are the right ones for our kids.

But for as many rough waters as we navigate, there are many blessings. Allow me to share some more about my beautiful Cassie. She loves to sing! She has performed at school talent shows, recitals, fundraisers, sporting events and has even been known to belt out some songs while in the middle of a store and entertaining all around her! Some favorites include All of Me, The Climb, Hey There Delilah, Bad Romance, Like a Virgin, In Case You Didn't Know, and many others crossing all genres of music. I am always amazed with the different songs she chooses. One of my favorite things to do with Cassie is to guess what song she is singing, because she usually doesn't start from the beginning. Cassie's dad ran the Pittsburgh Marathon blindfolded in 2013 and 2014 to raise money for different charities. In 2016, he pushed her in a stroller in the Pittsburgh Marathon while he ran. In 2017, Cassie ran the Pittsburgh Children's Marathon for one mile tethered to her father - and made ESPN's Top 10 Moments in Sports that same week! WTAE Channel 4 in Pittsburgh has produced several stories about Cassie, initially covering the marathon stories and then showcasing her love of singing.

My hope and prayer is that she continues to be a bright light in this world that is clearly sometimes very dark and a source of inspiration for those who may be facing their own challenges.

My intention for anyone reading my chapter is to encourage you to not limit your lifestyle because of challenges, yours or of your loved ones. Yes, you may encounter obstacles and bumps in the road, but that is every reason to grow and change from each experience as well as perhaps change others. If you are a parent of a child with a diagnosis, take the risk and do something out of the ordinary. And I encourage every parent of every child diagnosis or none, always do the right the thing. Teach your child to be kind to others. Preach that the world revolves around differences. Teach your child that everyone is different, and nobody is perfect.

Each child has a special place on this Earth, and in order to for the world to spin, everyone needs to understand that.

Meet Ausome Mom Jennifer Bruno

Jennifer is a mom of 2 girls, Carly and Cassie. She helped create Team Cassie, part of The Pittsburgh Foundation, to be help support local special needs families and children by providing grants for bicycles or activities. The first grant was awarded to the Western PA School for Blind Children and with continued fundraising efforts, the family hopes to be able to provide more grant opportunities to others in need. Jen continues to be an advocate for her daughter and is working with her local school district to provide some additional education to its staff and student populations. Jennifer works full time as a divisional director for a healthcare company. In her spare time (HA!), she enjoys reading and refinishing old furniture.

I Thought You'd Never Ask
Kelly Cain

"The first step to receiving an answer is being brave enough to ask a question." ~Anonymous

My legs were stuck to the leather seat. It was so hot on that August day, now forever known as "diagnosis day." We were stuck in Pittsburgh construction traffic, without air conditioning, on our way with our son to speak with professionals. We waited six months for this appointment, and we were anxious to get there. I was sure anxious to get there.

I knew something was wrong, and I needed someone to tell me how to help him.

Clayton didn't mind the traffic. He loved being strapped in tight while riding in a car. In fact, he did many things that just didn't add up. He couldn't sit in his high chair, on a couch, or in a recliner. He never looked anyone in the eye. I wanted someone to tell me why. The only time he would look at me is in the bathtub. I would actually feed him in the bathtub, and would just cry.

What was going on?

Clayton is our youngest child. Loved and doted on by older sisters, he never needed to ask for much, and always seemed like he just wanted to keep up with them. I knew though, I just knew there was something more.

The doctors said, "We don't worry till he is 3, Mrs. Cain, he is a boy. Mrs. Cain, he is fine."

25

I remember when he was 18 months old and it was Christmas morning - all those lights, all the presents, and that excitement of Christmas. He stepped over all the presents and sat down to play with the toys just like any other day.

I was prepared for this meeting today. They were not going to tell me he was "fine."

We finally made it through the traffic. We arrived on time, actually. We filled out all the paperwork and waited some more, of course anxiously. I was so afraid if I didn't answer something correctly or leave out any details about his behaviors or delays that we were seeing, that maybe they would tell us he is "fine" and "just a boy."

Two young doctors came in and began to go over our paperwork, verifying our answers, and going over our concerns. Clayton was laying on the floor, playing with trains. He never looked up to see who came in the room. The doctors started to whisper, excused themselves and came back. The one doctor said "Do you mind if I touch him?" We shook our heads no. He pushed on the back of his legs, up his back and even patted his head. Clayton never flinched. They tried to engage him.

"Is he always like this?" "Yes," I said. I have a list of concerns and examples, I said. "Mrs. Cain, was your pregnancy normal? "

"Yes. My first pregnancy was not, I was toxemic at 3 months, failed every blood test and had amniocentesis to rule out Down Syndrome."

"Really?" he asked curiously. "Yes. This pregnancy was easy."

Then ...

"Based on our observations and your concerns expressed we are sure of our diagnosis of autism."

Silence. We didn't look at each other. I didn't know and I knew my husband didn't know what autism was. My husband asked, "Will he have this the rest of his life?"

"Yes," one of the doctors said, "and he will probably never speak. This diagnosis will label him as disabled. You will need a service provider to coordinate services. He will also need state insurance because private insurance will not cover his therapies."

Disabled? Service Provider? Therapy? I asked, "Can you tell me how to help him?" "Mrs. Cain, you cannot help your son - he needs more than you. I am very sorry. The receptionist will give you all the information you need. Good luck."

Good luck?!

None of my questions were answered. Is autism why he only eats in the bathtub? Is autism why he doesn't look at me? We left with a huge packet, full of words I didn't want to learn or understand. Autism?

In the car, as my legs began to melt to the seat, I started to cry. Cry hard. Not understanding a thing, none of our questions answered, instead of getting clarity things seemed worse. I felt trapped.

We had no choice but to dive in. I had to learn the language of autism, specialists in my house, sensory issues, behavior therapy, sign language, special schools, and private schools. We were fighting for him to become verbal. We were learning how tiptoe through this world, observing him and learning his triggers. We were fighting to be a normal family of five. We were trying to explain something I barely understand to family, friends and to his sisters.

27

I went through the process of blaming myself. I went over my pregnancy in my head. What did I do wrong? What did I do different? What baby food did I feed him? What is in our water? What happened in three short years?

My husband said to me, "It doesn't really matter now, what matters is how we move forward." He was right.

We moved forward one step at a time, sometimes falling but always getting back up while questioning every decision. We were (are) constantly learning, not always from doctors or therapists. We learn from Clayton himself through the meltdowns in restaurants, meltdowns in school, all of the stares, all of the screams and all of the sleepless nights.

So often we have found ourselves splitting up as a family to go to events and to church. We didn't have a family outing for years. Sometimes, we still don't. The five of us have done more apart than together. The family strain is real and frustrating.

Clayton eventually started talking, at age seven to be exact. And finally at age 11, he made his first friendship. Speech and language therapy was our longest approach - he finished at age 13. We proved those first doctors wrong - he did speak, and I knew there was so much more he was able to do. We fought our way through school, for him to stay within typical classes, and even helped his teachers learn about autism along the way.

He is currently a sophomore in a mainstream school. Our son, who was never supposed to talk, stood up one day in his government class and gave an unplanned recap on current events. His teacher was so impressed, and he let all of Clayton's other teachers know. The administration heard about this accomplishment, and he was asked to give his story yes, his personal account of his journey with autism to professionals in the district.

I was apprehensive. The talking points were questions I had never asked him. "What was it like to have autism? What is it like to have sensory issues?" Sitting at the kitchen table, I wasn't sure he would be able to answer those questions.

To my surprise, he looked right at me, and started to explain in detail.

Just like that day in August, I was stuck in my seat at the kitchen table. Clayton talked for 15 minutes about autism, his sensory issues, overcoming barriers and what he thinks needs to change.

Stunned, I said to him proudly, "I can't believe you said all of that! I am so proud of you. I can't believe that's all in your head."

Clayton said to me, "I've just been waiting for someone to ask me."

He did accept the invitation to speak. That day, in front of 17 paraprofessionals, a young man who was told he would never gain verbal speech gave his story and shared his journey with autism.

Our son has overcome so much. I cannot wait to see and hear what else he does. He can now tell his own story.I will probably be stuck in my chair, and I will be the one speechless.

Meet Ausome Mom Kelly Cain

Kelly Cain from Pittsburgh, PA is currently a director at the Autism Caring Center which was founded in 2017. Advocacy, professional training, support groups and family activities are provided free of charge. She is also a founding board member of PALS (providing, assistance, love and support) a free recreational program approaching its 9th year of support for special needs families.

From Pain to Peace to Purpose
April Green

"Consider it pure joy, my brothers and sisters,
whenever you face trials of many kinds,
because you know that the testing of your faith
produces perseverance. Let perseverance finish
its work so that you may be mature and
complete, not lacking anything." ~ James 1 2:4

My husband Vondell and I had just finished enjoying a relaxing day together. Our three young children at the time aged two, three, and seven had spent their day with a close friend and her family. When we picked up the children, my girlfriend said this to me:

"Girl, you know she has autism right?"

Seven words I will never forget.

Seven words that shook me to my core.

I looked at her and said, "Yes, I already know. I am waiting for her to turn two years and six months old before I take her through an assessment. I want to give her a chance to grow."

My other two children were assessed through our local Child Find program. Both my son and my daughter were assessed at the age of three. My main concerns at the time of referral for the both of them were speech and language. My son did not qualify for services at the time, however, my daughter was diagnosed with a speech and language impairment. Little did I know that my daughter receiving that diagnosis was just the beginning of her journey with autism. Although my son did not qualify for services initially, that would not always be the case.

31

The ride home that day was the longest ride ever, both figuratively and literally. What normally would have been a 20-minute ride home turned into an hour and a half road trip. When we got to the car and began our drive home, I said to my husband, "you know she said she has autism."

As the words came out of my mouth, a heaviness filled the van. The hurt and confused look on my husband's face is something I will never forget. It was as if we were both in shock, or some kind of daze.

Did I see signs? Yes, I did.

Did I already know in my heart that my baby girl was living with autism? Yes, I did.

Although I already knew that there was something going on with her, it still hit me like a ton of bricks to hear someone say that my baby girl had autism. My baby girl was assessed at exactly two years and six months of age on August 19, 2014, one-day prior my 36th birthday. To date, that day was one of the most stressful days of my life.

At the time, my baby girl had limited verbal skills and her attention span was very short. She was so busy at the assessment that the team had a difficult time getting her to sit and attend to task. The team relied heavily on my observations and insight provided in order to determine her level of ability and functioning. She qualified for services in the areas of pre-academics, language and personal social skills and began to receive in-home support through the Infants and Toddlers Program. This program proved very beneficial in her attainment of early learning skills.

I believe that early intervention is critical. It is very important for your child to have experiences with others such as teachers and therapists to help facilitate their growth. Within two months of qualifying for services through the Infants and Toddlers Program, a developmental pediatrician assessed her for autism. Three appointments and five months later, my youngest child was diagnosed with autism. My husband and I were prepared for the diagnosis; however, you can never prepare enough emotionally to hear a doctor tell you that your child is living with autism. It is as if when you hear those words you can physically feel your heart breaking and balling up on the inside. I felt an immediate sense of loss and fear of the unknown. When you have a baby, you have hopes, dreams and aspirations for them and it was as if I was mourning the loss of those dreams, hopes and aspirations. All I felt was the pain, no peace, no purpose.

But God!

At the time that my youngest was diagnosed, I had no idea that within the next 18 months all three of my children would be diagnosed as individuals living with autism.

While my baby girl was receiving services at home, my middle daughter had begun to receive services at the local early childhood center for speech and language impairment. While receiving speech services, my middle daughter's teacher noticed some behaviors in her that caused alarm. The behaviors included having difficulty with change and transitions, not following directions, and problems self-regulating when upset. My son at the time was eight and was in the third grade. He, too, was having a very difficult time in school. He was very bright, but exhibited many behaviors that raised red flags, both at home and in school. He was a very fussy eater, exhibited severe test anxiety, he developed fixations, had a hard time accepting responsibility for his actions, became preoccupied with wearing a jacket and backpack, was oppositional, and demanded lots of attention from the teacher. He would often have meltdowns and had a designated classroom that he could go to when he could not manage in his own class.

As we went through the referral process for assessment for my middle daughter, autism was the furthest thing from my

33

mind. I said to myself "she talks, is very advanced far beyond her years and is very social, we just have some behavior concerns so she will just qualify for social-emotional help in addition to her speech services."

Boy, oh boy, was I wrong.

The psychologist who assessed my daughter was a jewel, and I will be forever grateful for her support. Prior to our meeting to discuss the assessment results, the psychologist sent me the report. I was sitting in my car, in the parking lot of a popular chain store, when I opened the report and began to read. I was in total shock when the assessment revealed that she was diagnosed with high functioning autism or what would have been diagnosed as Asperger's Syndrome in years past.

As I sat in my car in disbelief at what my eyes were reading, I cried my eyes out, pain and grief overcame me. Six months earlier, my baby girl was just diagnosed with autism, now my oldest girl.

"What is going on? Why is this happening to my family?" I sat in my car for thirty minutes before I could gather myself together enough to pull out of the parking lot.

As I reflected on the fact that my middle baby was now diagnosed with autism, I could not help but think about all of the problems that my son was experiencing due to him now living with autism as well. Initially, I had to fight for the school team to assess my son. "He is advanced," they said, "what do you want him evaluated for?" they asked me. For the atypical behaviors that he was exhibiting that did not make sense for a child with such advanced comprehension and academic skills, that was what! Thankfully, the teacher agreed that my son did exhibit some odd behaviors that warranted assessment from the school psychologist. As a result, my son was diagnosed with high-functioning autism and a 504 plan was developed to help support his needs within the general education environment. I experienced such a feeling of relief, finally an answer after years of wondering why he exhibited so many "quirky" behaviors, self-regulation difficulties and social struggles in school.

After the relief settled in, then it hit me: all three of my children were diagnosed as living with autism. Wow. The sense of grief and sadness was overwhelming. I had no peace, and all I felt was the pain.

Through the pain, I began to rely on my faith to help me find my peace. I found peace with knowing that my three babies were living with autism, peace with knowing that they all have differences that impact how they see the world and that other people don't always accept or understand that. I found peace in knowing that God would give my husband and myself what we need to pour into each of them. I found peace in knowing that although the road may be rough at times, that it is a rewarding road with purpose. It brings purpose to bring a sense of hope to others and purpose to bring awareness, purpose to support other families on their "ausome" journey, raising "ausome" people.

Meet Ausome Mom and Project Visionary April Green

Hailing from Capitol Heights, MD, April Green is a wife and mother of three children living with Autism Spectrum Disorder. A licensed minister, April has worked in the field of early childhood special education for the past 20 years and is currently pursuing her doctorate degree in educational leadership. April has a background in psychology and Curriculum Instruction and Assessment. She has a passion for early intervention and promoting awareness. This passion led April to host and produce a podcast, Keeping it Moving with April and Vondell, which focuses on shedding light on mental health and autism awareness. She has also created a blog, Ausome-Sauce, which chronicles experiences raising multiple children living with autism. April strongly believes that awareness is key for acceptance and is dedicated to being a vehicle for change while helping others find peace and purpose through the pain.

Cultivating A Spectrum of Possibility
(While Consuming Copious Amounts of Coffee)
Catherine A. Hughes

"I don't need an inspirational quote. I need coffee." ~ Random coffee lover

Ok, so maybe you aren't a coffee drinker. I'm not judging. Maybe I am a little, alright, you got me. Perhaps your preference is tea. Or maybe you drink water (and maybe you can poke me to increase my own healthy hydration). Me, I need my coffee, and I need plenty of it. Let's face it - no matter what hurdles are before you, you need coping mechanisms to effectively manage your stress, motivation to move forward, and experiences that simply give you a reason to smile. It just so happens that one of mine is coffee, coffee, and more coffee.

Like the beautiful, powerful, exquisite women who grace the pages of this book, I draw on not just my daily caffeine jolt, but strong conviction from deep down in my soul in order to continue to create a path not just for myself and for my son Christian, but for individuals and family members who have been impacted by autism as we have that I am so blessed to support through my calling (not career, but calling).

I remember exactly what I was wearing on April 19, 2001 - an orange polo shirt, khaki capris, brown suede boots, and a matching brown suede button down blazer. It was seemingly another day, another doctor's appointment. This time, it was with our endocrinologist. Following that appointment, my family tried to enjoy a meal before I had to head to work. That day, my parents (who helped raise my son as I was a young single mother) and I were told that Christian's tantrums, lack of language and peculiar behaviors couldn't just be a "boy thing" and that we needed to continue to seek answers.

I never made it home to call for help or make any appointments.

"… you are under arrest for terroristic threats, endangering the welfare of a minor, and simple assault on your son."

This statement was made by an officer who never read my rights. I was arrested and then jailed for four days in Downtown Pittsburgh after patrons and the manager of a local restaurant watched me trying to calm my son amidst a meltdown and then remove him from the premises. They interpreted what they saw as child abuse, not once thinking "maybe this mother needs some help" or "why is this child struggling so much."

Child abuser. The people standing around the restaurant lobby while I was in handcuffs repeated those words in my ear, over and over again. I can still hear them if I sit silently enough.

Fast forward 6 weeks …

"... Pervasive Developmental Disorder, NOS." Dr. Newman said to me,

"Wait, so … this is something he can grow out of, right? I can get him help? At least he's not on the spectrum. That's a relief. It's not my fault."

"Cathy …" he said gently. "No, this is not your fault. It's nobody's fault. But PDD-NOS … it is on what we call the spectrum. Cathy, your son has a form of autism."

At that moment, I felt everything around me disappear, like I was sitting in an empty white room with endless walls and time and space. I felt great confusion setting in, incredible sadness for my son's future, immense anger at my pediatrician for not believing me when I asked for help as I insisted something wasn't right, and guilt for feeling a slight twinge of relief.

Inspired, influenced, and impacted by more people than I can count - clinicians, teachers, doctors, and people JUST LIKE YOU (and yes, also more trips to Dunkin' and Starbucks than I can count and willingly admit), we have blazed a trail and we have defied many odds.

If you at all have ever felt, or still feel, as if your loved one's diagnosis is your fault, I want you to STOP what you are doing right now, look in a mirror and say, out loud ..."This is not my fault. This is who he (she) is." I also need you to say:

"My loved one is not broken. They are not defective. They have a different way of being. It is up to me to accept, act, advocate and always love."

And add this:

"My loved one is a gift - maybe their struggles are not, but their talents and their being are. And together, we will change the world."

Please, say these affirmations until you believe them.

There's a quote floating in the autism community that goes something like this: "this wasn't the trip I was expecting, but I love my tour guide."

Christian's journey through intensive years of ABA treatment, outpatient therapies, nutritional and medical interventions, and schooling has not just led him to a place of abundance that at one point seemed so uncertain, but also propelled me to create a powerful and rewarding career where I can graciously give back some of what was given to my family.

My son, as I write this chapter, just turned 21. With support from our "aumazing" village and his own fierce determination, he is a high school honor graduate who achieved scholarships and community accolades. He has held part time jobs, and is currently seeking a position helping the elderly by volunteering his time at a local facility and working with a job coach to hone in on his skills. He's also learning to drive. Oh heavens yes, mama needs plenty of coffee when Christian is behind the wheel of the new Jeep.

As for me, I am blessed to serve as the Director of Family Support and Community Engagement at Achieving True Self, an organization that provides home and community services (primarily ABA at the time this was written) to families. I am also the founder of The Caffeinated Advocate, a blog (and brand perhaps, all to be determined in time) that allows me yet another avenue to share our living, breathing story with others and bless them as I have been called to do.

"How do you do it (besides several coffee cups a day)?" I don't have a one size fits all answer for you. There is no secret sauce that is going to provide you with the recipe for you or your loved ones. The spectrum is simply that - a spectrum - and though we all walk on the same planet, our paths sometimes run parallel and won't always intersect.

What I can tell you is, to be gentle with yourself as you learn, as you cope, and as you find your way through the tunnel and seek the light. I promise you, it is there. Some days is it hard to see. I would be lying if I said all of our days were filled with sunshines and rainbows. They aren't. The lightning still strikes, the thunder roars, and the rain still pours.

But I promise you - supports, resources, and ultimately hope for tomorrow always exists. Put in the work, follow your heart and gut unapologetically, and you will discover rewards.

To you, dear reader, I salute (with what else ... my mug) and toast to your family's future, with incredible love and light.

Meet Ausome Mom and Lead Editor Catherine Hughes

Hailing from southeast of Pittsburgh, PA in a small town recently dubbed as "the most boring town in Pennsylvania," Catherine is an innovative storyteller and community strategist employed in leadership at Achieving True Self. Inspired by raising her son with autism, now 21, she has built a career providing comprehensive support and passionate advocacy for children, families and their surrounding communities. She is a servant leader who cultivates relationships with grace and grit to create, enhance, and promote services and programs that transform lives. She maintains a blog and social media platforms, called The Caffeinated Advocate, and is currently working on her second publication and first full book, "Imprisoned No More."

17 Years of Speech
Donna P. Lund

*"The only thing I do know is that my life is my
story and I want it to read the best way
possible." ~ Donna Lund*

Seventeen years of speech therapy.

That is really hard for me to wrap my head around. I came to
that realization a few months ago as my youngest son Brian
began private speech with a new therapist at a new center a
few months ago. As I sat watching my teenage son struggle
to pronounce sounds through the observation window, I saw
my adult life flash before my eyes. I saw images of my oldest
son Donny as a five-year old along with images of a younger
Brian and my daughters Nikki and Catie as they were
dragged along during those early years.

I thought to myself, "how can I still be here? How can this
be?"

Seventeen years is a long time. Even though I have not been
the student, I have absorbed as much about speech as my
sons during these countless sessions.

When "I" started speech I was a broken, traumatized young
mom. My sister had just passed away at a very young age and
I was barely functioning. I have a vivid recollection waking
up (if that is what you call lying awake until dawn, then
peeling my exhausted, grief-stricken body out of bed) the day
after we buried Cathy. I told myself that morning that all my
attention must be directed towards Donny now. He was five
at the time and I knew something was amiss. I knew some
type of intervention was needed and I thought speech was
most likely the appropriate starting point. I am positive he

42

should have started therapy earlier but at the time I could not face it. After all, these were the cancer years, not the autism years. I knew my limits and couldn't possibly process and accept that two of the people I love most in the world were struggling with very complicated and incurable conditions. That is how my relationship with speech therapy began. The cancer chapter sadly closed and the autism chapter sadly opened - almost to the day. I had no idea what was waiting for me in the upcoming years and baby Brian was not even a thought. Pretty unbelievable as I think about it.

I do not want to think about it though. Honestly, I wish I could forget.

Ironically, Donny's first therapist was named Kathy, something I took as a sign from my Cathy. She was going to be the new Kathy in my life and in my mind she was going to make all of Donny's struggles disappear. I latched on to her, as I have a tendency to do with special therapists and teachers.

It makes me feel safe. It makes me feel less isolated and that everything will be ok.

Over the years I have tried not to latch on as much for various reasons but to some extent I still do. That year I learned so much terminology: echolalia, expressive language, receptive language and auditory processing to name a few. I was doing my best to absorb so much new information while managing my grief at the same time. If I had the luxury of a crystal ball, I would have studied communication disorders in college. Kathy guided me and held my hand as she suggested to pursue further testing. It was obvious that Donny's delays were more pervasive than just language. I thought of her as my guiding angel sent to me from my sister, my guardian angel. In those days I thought somehow my sister was behind anything positive that happened in my life.

That may sound silly but it is how I managed to get through those difficult days.

Fast forward to 2019.

I am definitely not the terrified girl I was then. Besides being seventeen years older and probably the oldest parent in the waiting room, I am ... okay. I was not seventeen years ago. I was far from okay. For several reasons, I was devastated. Now, as I look around the waiting room I see myself in various stages, I see a young mom with two small children. One sitting on her lap and the other throwing himself on the floor. This mom is doing everything she can to redirect her child in the throes of a tantrum but failing. I see her stress; I actually feel her stress as my heart starts to race remembering the tantrums I lived through. Instead of looking away and acting like the episode is not happening, I smile at her and tell her it gets easier. I do not want her to feel judged like I always did.

I see another "me" - a mom with a son, just a bit older. He is unable to interact with the other kids and is consumed with a certain topic. He is perseverating (another word I have picked up along the way). She tries desperately to engage him in a different conversation to stop the repetition, but he is not having any of it. I see her anxiety. I feel her anxiety.

I was her.

The waiting room is much different than our first waiting room. Gone is the small toy box in the corner with used toys. The blocks, cars and books do not exist. Now I see iPads mounted on a circular table to keep the siblings busy and TVs hanging in the corners. Perhaps though the biggest difference in the waiting room is ... me. I am much more relaxed and I do not waste my energy worrying about Brian becoming a sideshow as he furiously stims on his ribbon. I let Brian just be Brian and find a seat. Years ago, I would have been on the verge of tears as I tried to pull something, anything, out of my bag of tricks to end his repetitive behavior. I am not concerned with what people think anymore. That concern in itself probably took years off my life.

As I look around at all the beautiful children, I wonder how their story will play out. My story did not play out exactly like I had hoped and prayed for. That's the kicker. We as parents are not in control. We can take our children to therapy and be the facilitator of their services. We can try center after center and approach after approach but it may not play out like we want or envision. I think that is the most difficult part. To my point, Brian had early intervention services starting at twenty months. He went to a special needs preschool and received what are known as wraparound services. He has had speech services for thirteen years and is loved to the moon and back but still would be considered nonverbal.

Is it all random? Is it all fate? Is it God's will?

I have spent countless nights torturing myself with those questions and cannot come up with anything. I realize now that these questions cannot be answered and actually do not even matter. The only thing I do know is your story is just that. It is YOUR story and must be accepted, plain and simple. Acceptance brings peace and I think peace brings fulfillment. I will never stop trying, that is not my point. Try everything, read everything, talk to doctors, psychologists and other parents. Why some kids progress further remains a mystery to me.

My seventeen years of speech has forced me to evolve and that is a good thing. I have grown into my role and accepted it. One of the most important things that I have learned is that my heart is comprised of layers. Each life altering experience I have had, has created a new layer and has made me who I am, who I am supposed to be. The layer created by the heartbreak of autism is slowly but surely being covered by a layer of peace and that helps me move towards the future. Make no mistake, I am not happy about this and seeing both of my son's struggle is not any easier. It has caused buckets

45

of tears, years and years of self-doubt, frustration and fractured relationships. However, I just know that this is my life. It is my story and I want it to read the best way it can. I try not to get too consumed with the future because I cannot seem to piece it together and it will drive me crazy trying to unravel what makes the most sense for our family. Instead I focus on the here and now – the only way out is through. It has gotten me this far and we will get through together.

Meet Ausome Mom Donna Lund

Donna is a wife, mother of four and loving advocate from Pittsburgh, PA. Both of her sons have ASD. Her contribution to the autism community in her early years focused on fundraising and she raised over $150,000 for Autism Speaks. In 2011, the Lund family was featured in a documentary, The Family Next Door. The film's mission was to illustrate the emotional impact of autism on families, and its influence has led to speaking engagements that focus on Donna's message of compassion. She has been invited to speak at local universities with special education teachers as well as at high schools (including annually at Mt. Lebanon School District as part of their curriculum) to promote professional development. Donna was a speaker at the Robert Morris University Educational Conference and a guest panelist for Representative Dan Miller's Disability Summit. In 2018, she launched her blog, Labeled to Lunderful.

How Will You Cast Your Stone
Patti McCloud

*"I alone cannot change the world, but I can
cast a stone across the waters to create many
ripples." ~ Mother Teresa*

In this journey of autism, we're all doing the best we can to provide meaningful lives for our children.

The truth is that my son, Jordan, was perfectly and wonderfully made by God. We're just trying to catch up to him. He is a huge presence in our lives – a smiling, laughing, goofy blessing.

Jordan can light up room with his smile. He loves to make us laugh. He has an endearing spirit that draws teachers and aides and care workers to him. For the most part, he is pretty easy-going. He loves to hang out with his sister, his Dad and his big extended family and friends. He can spend hours navigating YouTube and flipping from site to site without ever having typed a letter.

It's easy to show or talk about only the good. We've been doing it since Jordan was born. "We're good!" "Jordan's good!"

But I'd be lying if I told you that on some days it's harder to find the blessing than others. It's easy to control what we let you see on the surface. It's hard to be vulnerable and share the tough stuff. There are many days when I feel like I've failed Jordan in some way. I think to myself, "if we'd only done more therapy," or "tried one more time with the diet." The list goes on and on. You see, Jordan does not yet have the overcomer success story.

Jordan needs help with all daily living skills, such as showering, dressing and some assistance at mealtime. At 22 years old, Jordan is not completely toilet-trained. Jordan has a short attention span and must constantly be redirected to the task at hand which makes it hard to learn vocational skills. When he's frustrated, he hits or destroys things. He has no concept of safety or danger and must be constantly watched.

JORDAN DOES NOT SPEAK. NOT A SINGLE WORD.
He can't tell us what is wrong when he's hurting or sick, he can't tell us when he's bored or annoyed or frustrated. We've never heard him say "I love you." Not even once. On the rare occasion that he cries, it is absolutely heart shattering as we try to navigate what the real issue is and what he is trying to communicate to us.

Some days seem very long. When you are exhausted from lack of sleep and getting pinched or pushed and you're watching your beautiful child bite himself in frustration, it's hard to see the blessing.

When you sit in yet another IEP meeting at school and hear the same goals with just a little bit of progress from year to year, it's like a punch in the chest every time and it's really hard to see the blessing.

When you petition the court for guardianship of your child and they so easily agree because it's very clear that Jordan will need us to make decisions on his behalf for the rest of his life, it's hard to see the blessing.

When you look ahead and see so little opportunity for your child, it's terrifying. Jordan has been in treatment and therapy since he was three years old, and yet he functions more like a gigantic three-year-old.

But even on the darkest, most frustrating days, when the only thing you want to do is just close your eyes and go to sleep so that you can wake up and start again, there is thing called …

HOPE. We have hope that tomorrow will be better, that we can make tomorrow better, that tomorrow will bring new mercies. We have to hold on to hope for a better future.

After 22 years in this journey, I'm finally learning to trust my gut and to stop second-guessing myself. I've learned that not every treatment works for every child. You can pour your heart and soul (and a whole lot of money) into a treatment or diet and it might not be the answer for your son or daughter. I've also learned that sometimes things are meant to happen in their own time and that it's ok to go back and revisit something that didn't work in the past. Sometimes quality of life – for everyone – is what is most important. I've learned that the learning and the skills development doesn't end and just because they couldn't do it before, doesn't mean they can't learn it later. I'm getting way better at seeing the blessings.

Jordan is so smart. He loves to be with his peers. He is learning new skills every day and new ways to show what he knows. He has a huge crush on a girl named Rosa. He loves to tease his sister and hug us when we've been away from him. He loves to watch YouTube clips and Steelers videos and attend Pirates games. I have no doubt that he understands everything that we say to him and about him. He communicates with no words and he keeps finding ways to show us what he needs or what he knows.

Just like everyone, Jordan deserves a meaningful, purposeful life – whatever that looks like. He deserves to live as independently as possible surrounded by his peers. He deserves to find some type of competitive employment. None of that will be easy. He's going to need help and lifelong supports.

And he's not alone.

Over 70% of adults with autism are not employed or under-employed. There are tens of thousands of adults on waiting lists for waiver dollars that will allow them to access supports and housing. Many adults with autism, even those with higher level skills, require supports and services throughout their lifetimes to ensure success.

Legendary broadcaster and Hall of Fame football player Frank Gifford passed away a few years ago and his wife gave a beautiful tribute to Frank regarding his faith.

Regardless of all of the awards and accolades that Frank received in his life, he was most touched by a trip he took to Holy Land and the Brook of Allea which is where David slayed the giant Goliath. David was able to slay the giant because of the faith he had in his God. Frank brought home a stone and he kept it in his trophy room and he would take people in there and show them that stone. He would often give stones to important people in his life and challenge them by asking them how they would cast their stone in life? How would they affect others? What was their part in the bigger picture?

Autism is our Goliath!

Special education budgets are strained, there is a lack of providers for therapeutic services, thousands of young adults are aging out the education system and will need supports, care, places to live and places to work.

What's your part of the puzzle? How will you cast your stone? How will you help to provide that hope to families? How will we provide what our children need? It will take a huge village to help to provide a meaningful, purposeful life for the Jordan's of the world.

And so I ask you, if this resonates with you, please share your story. It's important and unique and it needs to be heard. If there is one thing that I've learned after years of advocating for Jordan at both a local and national level it's that legislators, policymakers, funders and county officials really don't know what our lives are like. And they really do want to know. Show and tell them what you go through on a daily basis. Share your successes and your frustrations.

If you can take your child to visit them at an event or at their local office, do that. Are you afraid that your child might be disruptive or exhibit some strange or aggressive behaviors? Let them see your loved ones for who they are. Are you afraid they won't be able to read your documents because your child flooded the kitchen counter when you were in the shower? Trust me that makes a big impact.

If you don't bring them, that's ok, too, but bring a picture with you. Feeling so overwhelmed that you can't fathom getting to someone's office to share your story? We've all been there. Send a text or email and be heard. There are many national and local organizations that make it very easy for you to fill in your information and hit send. You can even attend events where you can share your story. Cast your stone!

It's easy to get discouraged. It's easy to feel sorry for yourself some days. It's ok to cry in the car or the shower and let all that frustration out. But don't stay there too long. And don't waste that frustration and anger, use it for the greater good. Share your story!

Find a local organization and subscribe to their email lists. Find parents that are going through similar issues and make a point to get together in person or even in a Facebook group. I used to meet with a group of parents while our kids attended social groups together. Some of the best laughs I've ever had are with other parents as we share the absurdity of our situations along with all of the really interesting advice we've heard over the years. Those groups will be your lifeline to learning about services and treatments and funding sources. Then, find a group of friends who have no connection to autism and make it a point to get together with them. If someone offers help, take it. Find a way to get respite. We all worry about caretakers not understanding or being able to effectively care for our child. Remember though, you need to take care of yourself before you can take care of someone else.

Finally, please have compassion and empathy for all who are on this journey with us, respecting everyone's choices. Don't bash other organizations. Find your passion and what you want to support and let others do the same. We are all trying to do the best we can. We all have different experiences and are seeking different things.

Oh, and share your story. You have no idea who you might touch and in your sharing, you might encourage others to share. Autism can be a lonely journey, but it can also introduce you to some incredible individuals along the way.

After 20 years in this autism game, I know that change is slow. But our stories do make a difference and will create a better world.

Share your story. Find your tribe. Count your blessings. Cast your stone.

Meet Ausome Mom Patti McCloud

Patti McCloud and family have served in fundraising and advocacy efforts since 2000. She has served as the Family Teams and Corporate Fundraising Chair and as Co-Chair of the Pittsburgh Walk in 2004 and 2005. In 2008, she participated on a panel at the Autism Speaks National Leadership Retreat. In 2009 & 2010, Patti served as Community Advocacy Chair in PA. She helped secure Act 62 in PA and the passage of the federally funded Department of Defense Bill. She has chaired Dress It Up Blue and Chefs Create Pittsburgh, raising hundreds of thousands of dollars for Autism Speaks. She has been an active Board Member of their Pittsburgh Chapter serving in various capacities. Patti is employed with Pressley Ridge as their Family Support Coordinator. She lives in Mars, PA, with her son, Jordan, diagnosed with autism and intellectual disability and her daughter, Nicole, who attends the University of Kentucky.

Raising Authentic and "Ausome" Brothers
Sarah Parks

*"There's no person in the whole world like
you. And I like you just the way you are."*
~ Fred Rogers

"You aren't spending enough time with him."

"Nothing is wrong with him."

"He'll grow out of it."

It was Colby's delayed speech that had me reach out for early
intervention and developmental therapy. As he grew older, he
was still not making eye contact, responding to his name, or
talking. I filled out an autism screening survey at the
pediatrician's office at his two-year checkup which came
back negative. This was my first child. I was listening the
doctor.

He would constantly cry and scream in public restrooms
while I changed his diaper which I found so strange because
he didn't fuss at home when being changed. There was a lot
of rocking back and forth, humming loudly and self-injurious
behaviors also present. There were no reasons for these
outbursts that I could see.

"What is happening? What is wrong?" I would ask myself
and cry.

I felt like a bad mom.

I felt helpless.

The only way to console him was to leave wherever we were. I felt so embarrassed because I didn't know how to soothe my crying child. Were people thinking that I was a horrible and abusive mother?

Going out with friends became nearly impossible. I wouldn't be able to socialize because Colby was hyper and he would get into everything. Even to this day he is either sleeping or going 100 mph.

He would not listen to me at all. "Why can't I parent?" I would ask. People would say to me, "kids will be kids; stop complaining."

I didn't feel like I was complaining. I knew parenting was going to be hard, but not THIS hard. I had been around many children before having any of my own and I had never seen so much defiance and screaming from one child at one time. I would see many people out there far worse off than me, and their children didn't act out like this. "What am I doing wrong?" I would continue to ask myself, time and time again.

The invites to hang out with friends started to lessen drastically. I felt alone.

I felt depressed.

I began to avoid socializing, and isolated myself from social gatherings all together - as if those friends hadn't already isolated themselves from me.

His early intervention therapists suggested that I take him to the local Child Development Unit for a psychological evaluation. The first available appointment was in six months.

I sat there, pregnant with our second child, when the psychologist came into the room and said "your son has autism."

Two months later, I gave birth to our second child. A boy, who would later be diagnosed with autism as well.

Some people view the initial autism diagnosis as horrible, but I didn't. Immediately after receiving the first autism diagnosis I went home and did plenty of reading on the subject. It helped me to understand my son better. Being given the diagnosis answered a lot of questions that I had about his behaviors and why "typical parenting" wasn't working.

Now that we had a diagnosis, we could start to access the help and support that Colby needed so badly. The diagnosis didn't change him. He will continue being him, but now I would know how to help him. None of my friends at the time had a child with autism so I felt completely alone, isolated and lost. After the diagnosis the friends who had written us off didn't come back around. Even some family members were skittish about having received the diagnosis.

"Nothing is wrong with him - you just don't discipline enough!" This was the time that I needed support and help. I was getting very little from very few.

In time, I made new friends with fellow "autism moms" from the outpatient therapy waiting rooms, at the special preschool, and through local autism organizations. If it wasn't for hooking up with them, I would still be feeling alone, isolated and lost. These families have gotten me through some rough times, and vice versa. I am happy to say that some of them have become my best friends.

I couldn't have been happier when one of our Therapeutic Support Staff (TSS) assigned to our son shared that she was able to utilize sign language. With Colby still being nonverbal at the time that was a huge help. The wonderful Miss Nicki was the angel we needed. I will be forever grateful to her for helping my child and I to learn how to communicate with one another. I am also grateful to Variety,

The Children's Charity (located in Pittsburgh, PA) for giving Tyler, my youngest, the gift of voice by presenting him with his very own Augmentative and Assisted Communication (AAC) device to communicate his wants and needs.

I fear that some people think that I throw "autism" around to get personal attention. I know I'm not alone in that.

That is far from the truth.

I am trying to educate others and spread awareness to the public and to loved ones. I talk about the highs and the lows and everything somewhere there in between. "Being a parent is hard for anyone" is something that was said to me that has stuck. Yes, I agree it is hard, but add many significant needs and adaptations into the mix!

Having two children, one with zero words and one with limited reciprocal conversation skills, I have to be very vigilant. I've been called a "helicopter mom" and I don't think that I am. I let them have fun and explore. I follow them around to ensure their safety because they have no concept of danger.

One of my biggest fears is for them to come around the corner bleeding or seriously injured. They wouldn't be able to tell me how it happened. So how would I find out? An ER doctor would ask "how did this happen?" and my response would be a shoulder shrug followed by "I don't know."

YEAH. That would make me Mother of the Year.

Another fear of mine is that one or both of them will elope and wander off. When I discovered that the county we live in had a program to assist with easing that fear, I was overcome with joy. The program is called Project Lifesaver. Once you enroll, you are given a tracking device to wear either on your wrist or your ankle. If the individual should go missing, someone would just call 911, give them their identifying number, and the search will begin immediately.

Throughout the day, I literally have to be in two places at the same time almost constantly. One child is screaming, crying, and bleeding all over the place and while I am tending to that, his sibling is letting out blood-curdling screams because the screaming of his brother is hurting his head. The "typical" parent would say from across the room, "put that down" or "don't do that." For my children, I have to physically go over and redirect them hand over hand because they do not respond to the latter. One needs deep pressure and squeezes while the other may not be feeling well and want to be cuddled.

It is really hard to get anything done throughout the day. It is also very hard to discipline them. I often fight with myself about WHAT to even discipline them about. Are they acting out because of their autism, or are they just being a ... kid? I have two children, both with autism. What is "typical behavior," I don't even know.

Loud screaming makes them scream back in return, because it hurts their ears and startles them. Let's say that Tyler is crying in pain or anger. Colby then starts screaming along because Tyler's screaming is bothering HIM. We have noise cancelling headphones for both boys, but they don't help with all noises.

It's like my life is a battle, not an intentional one, but one nonetheless.

The more I read about autism and heard stories shared from my friends, the more I understood the reasons why my boys behave the way they do. Our lives changed after the diagnoses, but I now know what help they need to be their best selves. I know what I need to do, to say, and how to act toward them.

I am so proud of both of my boys. They have come so far with hard work. I just hope that spreading of awareness never stops.

These boys are my world, and I wouldn't change them. They are who they are.

Meet Ausome Mom Sarah Parks

Sarah Parks, devoted wife and mother of two "ausome brothers" was born, raised, and still resides in Pittsburgh, PA. An avid scrapbooking fanatic, Sarah grew up with a spark for helping others. She started young with Brownies in the second grade, became an alter server, joined her church youth group, enrolled at her local volunteer fire company as a teen, and assisted at a vacation bible school. Sarah has always followed a calling to serve and "be a good neighbor." Compassionate, giving, loyal and kind, this "ausome mom" fundraises for walks supporting local grassroots organizations, is engaged with her school's PTA, and facilitates connections to create awareness efforts including within her children's school district. Sarah is on a mission to share resources and experiences with anyone in need or who will listen - and while she's at it, will keep you smiling and laughing.

Patience and Perseverance
LaJuan Poole

*"Love recognizes no barriers. It jumps hurdles,
leaps fences, penetrates walls to arrive at its
destination full of hope."*
~ Maya Angelou

Aaron was born just after midnight on a Wednesday. His birth was the easiest of my three children. As he came into the world, I can recall him not making a sound. I immediately panicked and began asking if he was alright. I thought that all children cried when they entered the world.

Not mine.

I was assured by my sister, fiancé and doctor that my child was fine, just observing his new surroundings. After the nurses cleaned him off a bit, he was handed to me. He looked at me and I looked at him. The familiarity was instant. He was at ease and soon after went to sleep on my chest. This may have been the first indication that my child would be different.

But different how? It would take me 4 years to figure out the answer to that question.

Aaron and his brother are 22 months apart and similar in many ways. Aaron, like his older brother, did not meet developmental milestones. At 18 months of age, he did not say any words nor did he seem to recognize his name. Because I had already been through the same situation with his brother, I immediately called our local Child Find program to have him assessed.

He was subsequently placed in the Infant and Toddlers Program in the county in which we lived at the time. The therapist would come to our house a bi-monthly to help Aaron develop his language skills. Though progress was being made, it did not seem to have the impact that it had on his brother. By the time he was 3 years old and transitioning out of the Infant and Toddlers Program, there was still no mention of the word autism until our very last appointment with the Infant and Toddler Speech Language Pathologist. She brought the school psychologist to my home who conducted an informal observation of my son during his session. At the end of the session, I was told that he might be on the autism spectrum but that was it. No further direction, instruction or advice was offered.

I spoke to my child's pediatrician who suggested that we consult a developmental pediatrician. During the same time, he entered an early childhood intervention program in the local elementary school. I mentioned that it was suggested to me that he may have autism and was told that they did not classify children that young as having autism unless they had a formal diagnosis by a pediatrician. Not that it would make much difference in the classroom setting though, because he would receive the same amount of services based upon his current abilities and not his particular diagnosis. Still I wanted him to be seen by the developmental pediatrician.

When I called Children's National Medical Center to make an appointment, I was told that because he was a new patient, they only made appointments on one particular day a month. The 1st month after I was advised about the appointment setting rules, I completely forgot about the appointment and missed the day to make the appointment. The following month I remembered to call in on that particular day but had done so too late in the day and all of the appointments were filled. In the third month, I was determined to make the appointment. This was the only task that I aimed to accomplish that day and I did.

63

The only problem was that the appointment was eight months out. EIGHT MONTHS. I had to accept that appointment and was hopeful that someone would cancel and he could be seen sooner, but that did not happen.

In the meantime, Aaron received special education services as well as speech and occupational therapy at school. His skills seem to grow, although on a limited basis. He was well behind his typically developing peers.

Although an official diagnosis had not been given, there were several signs that seem to point to the fact that my child was on the autism spectrum. I can remember when he was three, being at my grandmother's house and her calling, "Aaron … Aaron … Aaron" because he was standing in front of the television. I walked over to him to get his attention so that he would move from in front of the TV.

She immediately turned to me and said, "I don't think the child knows his name." I assured her he did but could not explain why he did not answer. Another instance was that his father and I took him to an urgent care facility. After fervently resisting the physician's physical examination she gently suggested that he might have autism and that we may want to have him assessed.

One day, I took him to the playground with his younger sister. Another mother noticed his lack of verbal ability, and she also witnessed him hitting me (a recurring issue throughout his life). While our children played she mentioned that my son reminded her of her nephew … that had autism.

Because of the length of time it took for us to get in to see the developmental pediatrician, Aaron did not get a formal diagnosis until he was four years old. By then, it was no surprise to me. It seemed to be a recurring theme while we were waiting for the actual diagnosis.

When we finally received the formal diagnosis the only thing I remember thinking is, "How do I help my child?"

We left the developmental pediatrician's office with an action plan. Although he was getting occupational therapy and speech therapy in school, it was on a limited basis. The developmental pediatrician thought it best that we supplement his therapy with private services outside of the school setting.

Aaron, soon after his diagnosis, began speech and occupational services, which I believed was going to be the magic bullet for helping him to overcome his difficulties and have him performing more like his typically developing peers. The truth is, it was not a magic bullet. I was not prepared for how long it would take to see progress.

What I did not realize at the time is that Aaron did not operate according to my timeline and that he was going to progress at his own pace. He is meeting milestones, just not according to the timeline prescribed by me or anyone else, and I have to be okay with that.

When I look back throughout his life, it is "aumazing" how much my child has grown and learned during this time. Things that I thought he would never be able to accomplish; he is now doing with ease. Although he still does not converse with me, he is able to communicate his wants and needs. Things that many parents take for granted, move me to tears. He was five years old the first time I heard him say his name and six years old when he easily recites my name and the names of his brother and sister. He was ten years old when he first told me he loved me. At eleven years old was his first attempt at conversation by announcing to me, "Hi, Mommy … it's me, Aaron" when he entered the room. These words, although simple things, I had been waiting for him to say.

He has a very long way to go and I honestly don't know how much he will develop, but having Aaron has taught me patience more than anything else.

While he has grown by leaps and bounds since he was initially diagnosed as being on the spectrum, I would be remiss to not acknowledge the herculean challenges we face day in and day out. Despite the many challenges we face, I know that Aaron is truly an "aumazing" child and I am truly blessed to be his mother. Having him has taught me so much including patience and perseverance. I thought I had those qualities before Aaron, but I didn't realize how they could be tested.

I am not a perfect mother. I have doubted myself so many times. "Maybe I should I be doing more to help Aaron," or "maybe I am not pushing him hard enough," or "am I too permissive?" are all thoughts that cross my mind on a daily basis. '

But at the end of the day I know that I am doing the best job I can do with the information that I currently have. When new situations or information arises, we adjust and keep it moving.

Self-doubt and criticism do not have a place in my life. I know that we have raised a truly "ausome" and "aumazing" child. I am proud to see how far he has come, and I am excited to see where he can go.

Meet Ausome Mom LaJuan Poole

LaJuan Poole is a native of Washington, DC, currently living in a neighboring Maryland community. She is a dedicated mother of three, with her middle child living with Autism Spectrum Disorder. LaJuan is passionate about bringing awareness to autism and sharing her story with others in hopes to encourage those who are on the journey caring for those living with autism. LaJuan believes that by sharing her own struggles, it may help parents in similar situations realize they are not alone in their struggles and can help them in their own journey.

Proud of Our Adult Child and Her Good Life
Anne Shipps

"If I had known what our lives would be like now, I wouldn't have spent all those years worrying." ~A sentiment my longtime friends— friends we have known since our children were toddlers—share when we talk. I am not sure who said this first.

I am not saying that we have no worries and that we don't have concerns about the future, but I do know that my husband and I share the feelings of our close friends that we spent way too much time worrying about what would happen when our children who have autism become adults.

The time when Ruthie graduated from high school before she started vocational training and then working was a particularly difficult time for her and for us. When I say "difficult" I mean "crisis" --behavioral outbursts, seizures, a hospital stay one time. We know other families who have had the same experience during the transition to adult live. Ruth was approved for Developmental Disability Administration (DDA) services during that time of crisis, which lasted months. The other families I know who have been through this time of crisis have all emerged on the other side with better lives--different priorities, routines, structures.

At this time, we have established work-life schedules and routines. Our daughter Ruthie, like so many of her friends, has a life which is so much better than we could have imagined and infinitely better than what we feared.

And our lives are better and richer, too, in unexpected ways. Ruthie is 34 so many people."

She does not work Wednesdays and takes the bus to visit her 86-year-old grandmother, accompanying her on errands years old and enjoys life. So many people enjoy her. One of the local librarians told me, "You have no idea how much joy Ruthie has brought to or getting take-out for lunch at a local restaurant. My mother says that they are greeted wherever they go. "Everyone knows Ruthie," she says.

Ruthie is a federal government employee (GS-2) and works about 20 hours a week at the Clinical Center of the National Institutes of Health in Bethesda, Maryland. She has worked at NIH for about five years now, having acquired her job through the Project Search program, a federal program that creates jobs for people with disabilities. She had an office job before that but much prefers food service. She believes in the importance of preparing patient trays accurately and likes being able to move around. Besides, she loves the music they play. Having a meaningful job makes all the difference and I feel so fortunate that Ruthie is employed. I know others whose loved ones have not fared as well.

Ruthie takes the Metro train or bus to and from work and uses Lyft when the weather is bad or she is working overtime. She is currently living at home, but has friends who live in their own apartments. Ruthie plans to fill out a form and apply for her own subsidized apartment.

Despite little help or support from us, her parents, Ruthie quit her active involvement in Special Olympics (she still swims the mile at least once a week) and took up LGBTQ rights as her cause. She is now an active participant in a church in Dupont Circle, D.C. comprised of people who identify as gay as well as their family and friends. We have joined her church, and although we do not attend regularly we do participate in community events.

Ruthie definitely has a mind of her own and follows through when she decides on a direction. Through Ruth, we have met and learned to value as friends so many people with lives so unlike our own.

She receives Developmental Disability Association (DDA) benefits such as job coaching and Community Supported Living Arrangements (CSLA). She is also an active member, appointed by the Governor of Maryland, to the Developmental Disability Council (DDC) which provides community support to the DDA. She prepares thoroughly for each meeting, deciding which grants she wants to vote to fund. Ruthie participates on the transportation committee of the DDC, speaking up for people like her who rely on public transportation, writing to the board of the Metro when she has concerns. For example, she voiced concerns about the elevator not working at her Medical Center Metro stop, a real inconvenience for people with mobility issues or people with epilepsy (like her).

This Metro stop serves NIH and the Walter Reed Army Hospital for returning veterans and there are many people who use wheelchairs that use that station.

Ruth was five years old before she could answer the question "What is your name?" She started receiving special education services in a self-contained preschool class in Prince George's County Public Schools in Maryland, right outside of Washington, D.C. I had a hard time doing more than glance at comprehensive evaluations, IEPs, and progress reports. All of that "below the first percentile" reporting was depressing.

As she got older, it did seem to me that comprehensive evaluations, IEPs and progress reports were more accurate with a wide range of scattered scores and skills. I remember reading an article in graduate school that it is not uncommon for scores on standardized tests to rise as young children with autism grow older. When they are young, they are really not interested in participating in tests. But when Ruthie was young and I tried to say "but she does this at home," teachers were quick to look at each other and whisper "denial."

When Ruth was in elementary school and I was in my late 30s, I went back to graduate school at the closest public university in College Park, Maryland. While I was earning my masters in special education, I had a wonderful course on how to teach reading.

Using what I learned and Ruthie's love for American Girls (because I always go with her interests, there seemed to be no point in trying anything else), I taught Ruthie at home and her reading and comprehension scores went way up! We worked together for about 45 minutes a day. As a teacher and a parent, I would have to say that teachers do have knowledge and are teaching because of a calling to teach but we parents are and must be the first and best teachers. No teacher has 45 minutes a day for focused reading instruction with one child.

Being able to read and write has made a huge difference in Ruthie's life. She even had a short letter published in The Washington Post when she was in high school. She was mad that the education columnist said that students in Prince George's County should not be able to go to Six Flags on field trips.

Ruth writes letters and emails to many friends. We go through a lot of stamps, but through her we keep up with so many friends and relatives. An auntie of mine in Wales wrote to me that Ruthie signs her letters, "stay joyful."

I recommend doing whatever parents can to help their children read and write but, even more important, is the teaching of and the opportunity for sustained practice of daily living skills. Ruthie is freer and more employable since she can get from place to place by herself and take care of her own needs. Ruthie's two sisters—one older and one younger— often accompany her and/or talk with her often. I

71

know that they consider her when they think about their futures.

Other parents I know talk about having to hand on responsibility for their children to siblings who will at some time in the future become "parents." We value, treasure, and love how Ruthie's sisters make her a part of their lives and value Ruthie's independence. Both of Ruthie's sisters helped with the transportation training, helping her learn to use Metro trains and buses to get where she wants to go. As we age, I expect that Ruthie will rely more on her CSLA support services to help her function in the community, but nothing can replace family involvement.

I rely on my family and also on groups of people brought together because of caring for family members with disabilities. We understand, encourage, and support one another. I am on the board of our county chapter of the Council for Exceptional Children, a professional organization for special educators. Most of the other board members have a child or a sibling with a disability. Ruthie, my husband, and I participate in Faith and Light, an international movement composed of small prayer groups centered around our friends with disabilities. We have Faith and Light communities in 80 countries. Our Faith and Light meetings can get pretty silly and funny although at times we cry with one another.

Because of Ruthie, we are connected in many profound, loving ways with family and friends. Over the years, time in committed, purposeful relationships entwines and enriches.

Meet Ausome Mom Anne Shipps

A mother for over 35 years and a teacher for over 20 years, Anne Shipps is grateful for her family, her school, her friends, and her community. Over 30 years ago after husband Karl's active duty as a Naval submarine officer, the family moved to Prince George's County, Maryland, the closest Washington, D.C. suburb with the greatest stock of affordable housing so Anne could stay home with three active children. They "bloomed where they were planted" and their children, especially Ruthie who has autism and epilepsy, learned what they needed to get jobs and become independent adults. They have access to public transportation (Ruthie does not drive), great support services, and a good job for Ruthie. They have made many friends, especially friends who have disabilities or friends who have family members with disabilities, who "aumaze" them with their individual solutions to living good lives.

Who's There When It's Time to Blow Out the Candles

Holly Teegarden

*"The greatest gift that you can give to others is
the gift of unconditional love and acceptance."*
~ Brian Tracy

One of the feelings that you will find threaded through any autism family stories is the sense of isolation. It's common, and sometimes the isolation feels like it will swallow you whole. Your child is different and for many kids and even their parents, they don't know how to accept or handle it. My daughter in her own nature isolated herself and still does. It's her way of coping with things. It's not that she's unhappy; it's just that she feels more comfortable being alone.

As a parent of a child on the spectrum, you also deal with feelings of isolation. The issues that you're tackling with your child you can't really talk about with parents of typical children. If I were to tell my girlfriends when Sarah was young about echolalia or her obsessions with order, they would have felt sorry for me and that's not what I wanted. I would rather just deal with it alone.

Advocating for your child can become a full-time job, which leaves little to no time for socializing, even with your own spouse. You're living in a world where your child is isolating themselves for their own survival and you're doing it at the same time too. I think there is no greater example of this than the concept of birthday parties.

The dreaded birthday parties.

My daughter is 11, soon to be 12, and she has probably been invited to about 10 classmate parties total.

Maybe.

For years, the number was at a zero. Not one classmate. Can you imagine? As a parent, you want to shield them from the harsh realities of the world where they might feel unwanted or not loved by their peers. And what would stink is I knew that my daughter knew about the parties going on around her. She would tell me that everyone is going to this person's party.

Everyone, but her.

Part of me would want to call the parents and shout, "WTF, people?" I get that my kid might talk to herself or blurt things out but still, have a damn heart.

If you're reading this and have a child in elementary school, please do me a favor and invite everyone to your next birthday party. Don't leave kids out just because they're "different."

To combat this void of not being invited to other parties, we would make OUR birthday parties BIG! When my new husband got on the "big party train" he was like, "you do this every single year?" Yes, sir, like a boss, I said.

I'm sure other parents were probably thinking, what are these people, moneybags? They are always throwing some elaborate event that was fun and everyone would be invited. I literally didn't care what the cost was when it came to her party. I know that seems nuts to many people. Our hope was that they would see Sarah as just a "normal kid" and the parents of her peers would perhaps be empathetic and explain to their kids that different is okay. I'm sure some of you just read this paragraph and said, she was trying to buy friends for her child.

Yes, yes I was. It's sad that I felt I needed to do that.

I do want to say that Sarah, in time, did start to receive party invitations. God bless neighbors and friends of our family, because she finally was invited to their children's birthday parties! The invites weren't mercy invites, but invites from those who truly understood Sarah and enjoyed being around her.

I want to share with you a little bit about the first birthday party that she ever attended. She doesn't remember, but I can tell you that I remember this day vividly.

It was 2011. Sarah was 4 years old and recently diagnosed with PDD-NOS. We got her into music and movement classes with this sweet mom whose son was also in the class. Sarah during the class enjoyed the music, but made very little eye contact, didn't speak, and kept to herself. We didn't realize just how different she was until we started putting her into group situations like this. Imagine our surprise when Sarah got an invite for the son's 5th birthday party. The party was at a local park. Low key. We thought, this is going to be great! She loves going to our park and always has fun.

When we got there, Sarah didn't want to play with anyone. Or speak to anyone. She would sit alone in different areas or wander off completely from the party heading towards the woods. My ex-husband and I had to stay vigilant watching her and not socialize with the other parents the whole time.

Remember at the beginning of this chapter about isolation? This is it folks, slapping in your face. Parents focused on their child, not talking to any other parents, and the child lacking social and verbal skills themselves.

I remember in the park talking to my ex-husband. It hit us just how different Sarah was from the rest of the kids. It was gut-wrenching to watch her - and watching ourselves - with the rest of the party going on. But wait, it gets worse! When the cake came out and everyone was gathered around to sing happy birthday, where was Sarah?

76

Under the picnic table. Everyone around it, and her under the table, hands over her ears and just rocking.

That was the first time my heart broke over her autism. We left right after that. It was sensory overload for her and we just weren't educated or equipped to know at the time that was what was happening. I remember getting in the car and just crying with my ex-husband. I'm talking SOBBBBBINGGG.

We thought, this is our future forever. Our child not able to function with other kids her age and being singled out, and us being frazzled forever running behind her to "save her." I think about the idea of isolation and there are just so many layers with birthday parties.

Flash forward. There's hope with all of this. I don't want to be Debbie Downer.
Sarah has come into her own and she'll throw up deuces to anyone who doesn't like her. But for a long while, our reality was like how I described above. Sarah will be 12 this year and this will be the first birthday that we won't do all the fanfare. She has found her tribe with two girls, and that's enough for her. It's enough for her dad and I too.

One of the things that I wanted to do in my chapter is to make sure I help parents like myself struggling with birthday isolations. Here is my advice:

1. First of all, I want to make sure that parents know that they're not alone. It helps to talk to other parents in your community that have kids on the spectrum. Find YOUR PARENT TRIBE because y'all are going to be together for a while.
2. I would reach out to the school counselor and your PTA/HSA and ask them what type of education they could offer to kids and parents about autism.

3.Get involved as much as you can at school functions. The more parents get to know you, the better it will be for your child.
4.In terms of birthday parties, be PREPARED!
  a.Figure out the roadblocks ahead of time with food choices and/or sensory overload either at their own party OR at the one they're going to attend.
  b.Accept what's going to happen is what's going to happen. It will not be the end of the world.
  c.Don't have any expectations of what a birthday party is "supposed to be" or how your child is "supposed to act."
  d.Stay at the party your child is going to and always have an exit plan.
  e.Give the hosting parents a heads up about how your child acts and what they might need.
  f.Contact the venue of the birthday party (whether it's your child's birthday or the friend's) and talk to them about their ability to accommodate children on the spectrum.

You're going to get through every birthday. I promise you that. Some of them may be harder than others, but as long as you stay positive, don't expect too much and fill them with love, you'll be … "aulright.".

Meet Ausome Mom Holly Teegarden

Holly Teegarden is a digital marketing consultant, national speaker on social media and analytics, autism advocate, digital detox expert, certified Christian Life Coach and doTERRA Wellness Advocate. She sounds busy (I AM). She lives in Sewickley, PA with her husband and her daughter Sarah. Holly is active in her community as the co-founder of the Quaker Valley Quaker Valley Special Education Parent Networking Group and with her church, North Way Christian Community Sewickley Valley. Holly has a degree in English Literature from Nazareth College in Rochester, NY. She dreamt of finishing college and writing for a living. This book is the start of that dream coming true.

KJ's Autism ... A Mother's Inspiration

Lenore Wossidlo

"It's tough, living with a sibling who has autism. Sometimes you wish they didn't have autism. Sometimes you wish that you were a single child. But in the end, you always love them. No matter what they do, no matter how they act, through the toughest times, the bonds of family will keep you and your sibling with autism together."
~ Paul J. Wossidlo, Age 15
(now a college freshman)

Karl Joseph (KJ) Wossidlo was diagnosed with autism on September 25, 1995. I remember it well because it was Yom Kippur, the holiest day of the Jewish religion. We should have been celebrating the New Year and this was how it started—with a diagnosis of autism.

October 25, 1986 was our wedding day. We were so excited, nervous, and happy. It was a rainy day, with lots of sunshine at the Holiday Inn in Braddock Hills, the site of our wedding and reception. We met on August 18, 1985, and our first date was August 25, 1985. It was love at first sight, and we became engaged four weeks later! Our son, Karl Joseph (KJ), was born on Monday, December 14, 1992, at 6:40 a.m. I went into labor at 1:30 a.m. He entered this world quickly.

KJ had his days and nights mixed up for about a year. KJ had to be completely asleep before I could put him in the crib. I would walk him to sleep between 1 and 2 a.m., while watching reruns of Maude, The Golden Girls and Cheers, as well as The Weather Channel. Today, TWC is his transition channel when he gets up, when he leaves the house, when he comes home, and in other situations.

After the shock wore off and we started down the path of teaching KJ, I learned sign language to help us communicate. Today, he knows more than I do. I have also taught him some of the Jewish prayers in sign language, which we now will sign at the Mostly Musical Shabbat services on the 1st Friday of each month. KJ hears and understands everything we say (sometimes too much). He needs help to answer us and to express his feelings.

When I am having a bad day, KJ comes over to me and hugs and kisses me. Even if his behavior is the reason for the day not going so well, how can I refuse that?

It has been said that GOD gives you what you can handle. GOD trusted us a lot! One month after we were married, my mom died very suddenly. I was absolutely devastated. This is the person who raised me, in whom I confided, whom I loved so dearly, who saw me so happy on my wedding day. We planned to have her live near us so we could take care of her as she grew older. "WHY," I asked GOD, "did you take her suddenly?"

Looking back, GOD wanted to have a very special mom in heaven, even if the timing was not good for us. Six years later, he gave us a child with special needs whom we could take care of and prepare for a productive life. KJ had a dairy intolerance for about a year and a half. Because I loved nursing him and he loved it, I had to keep cheese, milk, and other dairy products out of my diet for that year. Today, he loves all of these products and eats them without any side effects.

KJ started walking at 14 months and talking at 18 months. He only said a few words, with Mama being the first word he said. We were not concerned too much because I was a late talker, and I knew that every child reached milestones when they were ready.

81

I do remember the pediatrician asking me what words he said at 18 months; it was only five words. He asked me again at the 2-year visit what he said, and I was speechless.

KJ said no words.

He said that we should wait six more months, since he might be a late talker. At his 2 ½ year visit, the pediatrician gave me a prescription and contact information to start services. We did not know how to talk about it, what to talk about, or how to feel. We had no comparison, since KJ is our first child. However, we trusted our pediatrician to guide us, since he quickly picked up on the autism.

Music would soothe KJ, so we had calming cassettes and CDs in the car when we took him out. If we were indoors and he fussed, I would sing to him to calm him down. That was until he realized how bad my singing is! Then he would cover his ears because of my singing voice. He loved car rides, and today he is a fabulous passenger!

My husband Paul and I had known for some time that something was wrong. The language disappeared, and he could not tell us what he wanted. He didn't point or gesture, and he cried a lot, even if I left the room for a few seconds. Bright neon colors and loud noises bothered him. He was frustrated and did not nap! He would go-go-go for 15 straight hours! His record is 19 straight hours without a nap.

Our concerns led us to Karleen Preator at Children's Hospital CDU in Pittsburgh. I remember driving home on Rt. 79 in tears thinking, what next. What lies ahead for us? It took me many years to be able to drive on that part of Rt. 79 without tears.

Two weeks after the diagnosis, Dr. Preator met with us to discuss the diagnosis and how to proceed. This helped us so so so much, for now we had a starting point. She also encouraged us to BELIEVE in KJ's future, which we did!

KJ started attending a toddler group and then transitioned to PLEA preschool in January 1996. He needed structure; could he handle 5 days a week, 5 hours a day? Could I?

PLEA felt just right for us. Their staff felt they could help him, and three months after he started there, he was communicating with pictures! This is how we knew that KJ was extremely visual. PLEA was his foundation for his success today.

About two weeks after he started at PLEA, I got into my car after dropping him off and started bawling my eyes out. My baby's going to preschool, he has a backpack, and I packed him a lunch - major accomplishments!
When life's challenges have taken over, I ask GOD to show me the way. And if it is not the time, I ask him to show me a sign that it all will work out, just to keep me feeling positive. HE does show me the way!

Why is this important? Because you will have so many more challenges and questions along the way. You will cry, scream, wonder, laugh, smile. ASK FOR HELP; IT'S OKAY! It is a sign that you need help and you recognize its time to ask!

Looking ahead and planning for future services should always be on your radar. What is the next step for your child? Always think, what if? What is the best situation for MY child? How will MY child learn best and how do we make that happen?

In many situations, kids with autism cannot generalize. They think, "I do this only at school. I do this only with staff." If services are not working for you, think outside the box and speak up! Find out why they are not working and what can be changed to make it work. Sometimes the change can be something as little as how your words are phrased. This is your child and you are their advocate!

KJ and PJ

We always wanted two children, no matter their gender. We waited until KJ was in school full time to have another child.

On March 5, 2000, Paul Joseph Wossidlo (PJ) was born. I was sitting on the porch with PJ when KJ got off the school bus. I thought KJ was saying "bye" to PJ, as if to say, go back. I said to KJ that he was staying and that this was his baby brother. When I think back about that moment, he was just waving to PJ to say hi.

One of the challenges we faced as PJ got older was giving him enough quality time without KJ. We learned this by trial and error basis, and we communicate with PJ and LISTEN to his concerns. We work as a family team to resolve issues.

It is a daily juggling act, balancing our work schedule with KJ getting on and off the ACCESS bus. I have hand-to-hand services for him, meaning that the ACCESS driver must pick up and drop off KJ to a person, not just at the front door.

PJ is still understanding and handling KJ's unique needs. He defends KJ and even sometimes will help ME stay calm. I remember one time when KJ was coming home and walking up the porch steps (with one of his aides). PJ and I were next door, along with some other neighbors. One of the kids started laughing at KJ. PJ said, very emphatically, "don't you laugh at him; he is my brother!"

KJ tries his best to be a "big brother" to PJ. He knows it is hard because of his autism. He has apologized to PJ many times. All he really wants is acceptance from PJ, and everyone, as to how unique he is.

KJ's Bar Mitzvah

As KJ approached 12, and I realized he would be 13 the following year, thoughts about his Bar Mitzvah came to mind. This would be challenging. How would we do it? Who would come? We discussed with our Rabbi the importance of this, to KJ and to us as a family. It was important to us because I felt it would bring us together in a way that no other event could. I would help him prepare.

We enrolled him in a religious school for special needs. We discussed with the Rabbi what the important parts were for him to consider it complete. We laid out a plan to prepare KJ with the four items that would make it official. This included rehearsals, making a picture schedule for the congregation to see and a smaller one for KJ to use, and deciding who would be invited. This needed to be a small event. I had help from several individuals and a couple of Jewish organizations.

On Sunday, August 20, 2006, KJ celebrated his Bar Mitzvah, with sign language and pictures, in front of very close family and friends, many of them with autism. We had a small reception afterwards, and we breathed a sigh of relief! We were very proud of our son with autism, for accomplishing this major task.

Community and Law Enforcement

When I realized how strong KJ was at age 5, I thought to myself, what if he hit a police officer? Would they understand? In 1998, my ongoing project began to help law enforcement understand the characteristics of autism, tips on how to recognize it, and suggested ways to handle situations. Our neighbors know and understand KJ well and could help in an emergency.

This was so well received in the law enforcement community! Police officers, fire departments, and emergency service personnel want to know this information. I spoke to my local police department in Swissvale. This led to a television appearance and newspaper articles, as well as many presentations.

Making your local first responders aware of your child with special needs will help immensely if any emergency were to occur. Think ahead, what if this happened? How would they respond? How would my child respond? What do I need to do or to tell a first responder in order to have a more positive outcome?

With the help of several police departments and Woodland Hills Theater Department, I produced a videotape illustrating different scenarios, details about the scenarios, and suggested ways to handle them. The police departments also helped me to make copies for Allegheny County police departments and the PA State Chiefs of Police Convention in Lancaster, PA. It is critical to have an information form on file with your local police department, as well as police departments in the areas that you vacation in, and a brief form in the glove compartment. I say brief because they need the info as quickly as they can get it. Make sure you tell the dispatcher that there is someone with autism involved in the situation in which you are calling about. Check with your local police department or online for police forms for individuals with special needs.

It is sometimes necessary to have stickers and/or magnets on your car windows and bumpers that say, "child with autism; may not respond to verbal commands." You can add "non-verbal." This will help them to be more prepared and that they may have to think outside the box.

Wednesday, our therapy cat, came to us in June of 1999. My sister-in-law purchased a gift certificate for us from the Western PA Humane Society, after our very first cat Cuddles crossed over the rainbow bridge in November 1998.

We went to the Western PA Humane Society to give a cat a home. I walked into a room full of cats and kittens who needed homes. This one black cat tapped me on the shoulder with her paw. I turned around and said "hello." We read her bio sheet, and it said that she is a lap cat and is great with kids. The volunteer told us that she works well with kids with autism. There was a school in the area who would bring their kids there every week to spend time with her. There was our answer who was coming home with us - Miss Wednesday, a.k.a. Princess. She had been at the shelter for two years. She crossed over The Rainbow Bridge in 2015, forever in our hearts. We now have another black cat, Wednesday 2. KJ loves the cats, especially the calmer ones. He loves to pet them. We have shown him how to pick up the cats when he needs to move them. I always bring up a cat to say goodnight to KJ.

Today

Wednesday, May 29, 2014, KJ walked across the stage with his diploma from Spectrum Charter School. A major goal was accomplished. Spectrum Charter School looked for the skills in KJ and helped him to excel in those skills still holds the record of folding 170 boxes in 2 hours at the Westmoreland County Food Bank. In May of 2008, KJ was named Volunteer of the Month for his packing, stacking, and moving boxes of food in a timely manner.

He now works full time at Milestones Prevocational Center in Monroeville, PA and loves working! He is still getting used to shorter holiday breaks and working in the summer. We are also realizing that just like everyone else, he needs holiday breaks and a vacation. KJ also enjoys playing Miracle League baseball. I believe he loves it because he has played baseball on the Wii for many years.

KJ's autism is truly a mother's … my … inspiration.

Meet Ausome Mom Lenore Wossidlo

Lenore Wossidlo lives in Pittsburgh, PA, with her husband Paul, her sons Karl Joseph (KJ) and Paul Joseph (PJ) and her cats. She has been an advocate for autism for many years, marching on the steps of the Capitol Building in Harrisburg when Pennsylvania wanted to make changes to the Medical Assistance program and cut services. She has participated in walk-a-thons for autism and has spoken to many police departments and associations about autism for emergency responders. She promotes awareness about autism's characteristics and offers suggestions to produce a positive outcome. Her inspiration for writing comes from her late grandfather, Dr. Joseph H. Greenberg. Her determination and persistence in life comes from her late mother, Sylvia G. Sadwick.

Ausome Autism Resource Center

Advancing Futures for Adults with Autism:
www.afaa-us.org

AIMS
www.aimsinstruction.com

American Academy of Child & Adolescent Psychiatry:
www.aacap.org/aacap/families_and_youth/resource_centers/
Autism_Resource_Center/Home.aspx

American Occupational Therapy Association:
www.aota.org/About-Occupational-
Therapy/PatientsClients/ChildrenAndYouth

American Speech-Language-Hearing Association:
www.asha.org/public/speech/disorders/Autism
www.asha.org/Practice-Portal/Clinical-Topics/Autism

Autism Asperger's Digest:
www.autismdigest.com

Autism Navigator®:
http://autismnavigator.com

Autism NOW:
https://autismnow.org/

Autism Society of America:
http://www.autism-society.org/what-is/

Autism Speaks:
www.autismspeaks.org

Behavior Analyst Certification Board:
https://www.bacb.com

Changing Spaces:
www.changingspacescampaign.com

Faith and Light:
https://www.faithandlight.org/

National Autism Association:
http://nationalautismassociation.org/

The Autism Community in Action:
https://tacanow.org/

Understanding Autism, The Basics - WebMD:
https://www.webmd.com/brain/autism/understanding-autism-basics#1

Continue to Follow Some of Our Author's Journeys:

Ausome-Sauce:
https://ausomesauce.wordpress.com/

Autism Caring Center:
https://autismcaringcenter.com

Everyday Life Coach:
https://open.spotify.com/show/2M6VHKVwR6TQseu7wPbl
gm?si=CKs4UH1ZQPaQwScmuHsRzg

Keeping it Moving with April and Vondell:
http://streaminginspiration.net/?page_id=29896

Labeled to Lunderful:
http://www.labeledtolunderful.com

Living in Boldness:
http://livinginboldness.com

Love, Hope & Autism
https://www.facebook.com/LoveHopeandAutism

Team Cassie Fund
https://pittsburghfoundation.org/team-cassie

The Caffeinated Advocate
http://caffeinatedadvocate.blogspot.com

Bibliography

CDC's Autism and Developmental Disabilities Monitoring (ADDM) Network, Division of Birth Defects, National Center on Birth Defects and Developmental Disabilities, Centers for Disease Control and Prevention https://www.cdc.gov/ncbddd/autism/data.html, November 15, 2018.

Contact

For more information and booking, please email our
Ausome Moms at itsgoingtobeaulright@gmail.com